MAKE YOUR OWN
BALLOON-POWERED CAR

BY CHRISTOPHER HARBO

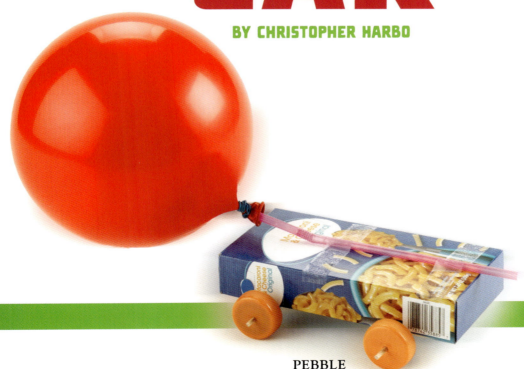

PEBBLE
a capstone imprint

Published by Pebble, an imprint of Capstone
1710 Roe Crest Drive, North Mankato, Minnesota 56003
capstonepub.com

Copyright © 2026 by Capstone. All rights reserved. No part of this publication may be reproduced in whole or in part, or stored in a retrieval system, or transmitted in any form or by any means, electronic, mechanical, photocopying, recording, or otherwise, without written permission of the publisher.

Library of Congress Cataloging-in-Publication Data is available on the Library of Congress website.
ISBN: 9798875225123 (hardcover)
ISBN: 9798875225017 (paperback)
ISBN: 9798875225086 (ebook PDF)

Summary: Experiment with wheels and axles and forces and motion with this fun project! Gather simple supplies, follow the steps, and watch the car zoom away.

Editorial Credits
Editor: Erika L. Shores; Designer: Heidi Thompson; Media Researcher: Jo Miller; Production Specialist: Tori Abraham

Image Credits
Capstone: Karon Dubke: all project photos, supplies; Shutterstock: CHARAN RATTANASUPPHASIRI, 5

The publisher and the author shall not be liable for any damages allegedly arising from the information in this book, and they specifically disclaim any liability from the use or application of any of the contents of this book.

Any additional websites and resources referenced in this book are not maintained, authorized, or sponsored by Capstone. All product and company names are trademarks™ or registered® trademarks of their respective holders.

TABLE OF CONTENTS

Vroom! Vroom!. 4

What You Need. 6

What You Do 8

Take It Further 20

Behind the Science. 22

Glossary 24

About the Author 24

Words in **BOLD** are in the glossary.

VROOM! VROOM!

Cars need **energy** to run. Most get their power from gasoline or electricity. But can a car be powered by a balloon? You bet it can! Gather a few simple supplies to make your very own balloon-powered car.

WHAT YOU NEED

- scissors
- large straight straw
- tape
- small pasta box
- wooden skewer
- large nail
- 4 plastic milk caps
- bendy straw
- balloon
- rubber band
- an adult helper

WHAT YOU DO

STEP 1

Cut the large straight straw in half.

Tape both straw halves to a wide side of the pasta box. The straws should be **parallel** to each other and near the ends of the box.

STEP 2

Ask an adult to cut a wooden skewer in half.

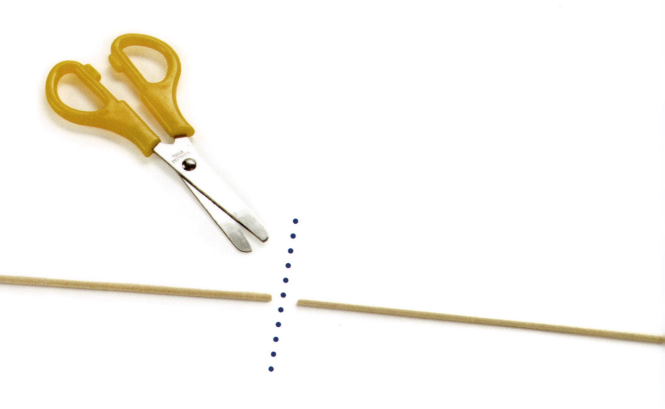

10

Slide each skewer half through the straw halves taped to the box.

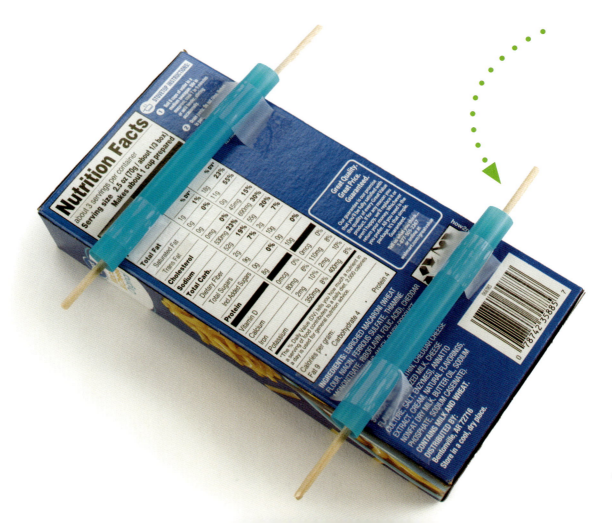

11

STEP 3

Ask an adult to make a hole in each milk cap using the nail.

Slide the milk caps onto the ends of the skewers to make wheels.

Turn the car over.

STEP 4

Insert the short end of the bendy straw into the neck of the balloon.

Wrap a rubber band around the neck of the balloon to hold it tightly to the straw.

STEP 5

Tape the bendy straw to the top of the car. Allow the open end of the straw to hang off the back of the car.

STEP 6

Blow into the open end of the bendy straw to blow up the balloon. Once full, place your finger over the end of the straw to trap the air.

Set the car on the ground and remove your finger. Watch your balloon-powered car zoom away!

TAKE IT FURTHER

Do the materials you use to build your car change how fast it moves? Try building your car out of candy boxes, paper towel rolls, or soda bottles.

Does the new car you made go faster? Build several cars and hold races with your friends!

BEHIND THE SCIENCE

All cars need energy to move. The car you made gets its energy from air. Taking your finger off the straw lets the air inside the balloon shoot out. This **force** pushes your car forward.

Your car is an example of Isaac Newton's third law of motion. This law says that for any **action**, there is an **equal** and **opposite reaction**.

GLOSSARY

action (AK-shuhn)—something that is done to achieve a result

energy (EN-er-jee)—power from gasoline, electricity, or other sources that makes machines work

equal (EE-kwul)—the same as something else

force (FORS)—any action that changes the movement of an object

opposite (OP-uh-zit)—facing or moving the other way

parallel (PA-ruh-lel)—to be in a straight line and an equal distance apart

reaction (ree-AK-shuhn)—an action in response to something that happens

ABOUT THE AUTHOR

Christopher Harbo is a children's book editor from Minnesota who loves reading and writing. During his career, he has helped publish countless fiction and nonfiction books—and has even written a few too. His favorite nonfiction topics include science and history. His favorite fiction books feature superheroes, adventurers, and space aliens.